YOUR
GROWING
BODY
and
Remarkable
Reproductive System

FIND OUT HOW YOUR BODY WORKS!

Paul Mason

Crabtree Publishing Company
www.crabtreebooks.com

Crabtree Publishing Company
www.crabtreebooks.com
1-800-387-7650

Published in Canada
Crabtree Publishing
616 Welland Avenue
St. Catharines, ON
L2M 5V6

Published in the United States
Crabtree Publishing
PMB 59051
350 Fifth Ave, 59th Floor
New York, NY 10118

Author: Paul Mason
Editorial director: Kathy Middleton
Editors: Annabel Stones, Shirley Duke, Kelly Spence
Designer: Rocket Design (East Anglia) Ltd
Consultant: John Clancy, Former Senior
    Lecturer in Applied Human Physiology
Proofreaders: Susie Brooks, Rebecca Sjonger
Prepress technician: Margaret Amy Salter
Print and production coordinator: Margaret Amy Salter

Published by Crabtree Publishing Company in 2016

First published in 2015 by Wayland
Copyright © Wayland, 2015

Picture credits:
Getty Images: p15 br The Washington Post / Contributor, p29 br Jeff J Mitchell / Staff; Science Photo Library: p7 cr, p15 tl JACOPIN, p17 bl PIXOLOGICSTUDIO, p18 JACOPIN, p21 tl PETER GARDINER, p23 cl STEVE GSCHMEISSNER, p25 bl STEVE GSCHMEISSNER; Shutterstock: p3 t, p3 ct, p3 cb, p3 b, p4 tr, p4 br, p5 t, p5 cl TonyV3112, p5 br, p6 l, p6 br, p8, p10, p11 t, p12 cl, p12 b, p13 cr, p14, p17 tr, p17 br, p19 tl, p19 tr, p19 br, p21 tr, p21 bl, p22, p24, p25 t, p26 l, p26 r, p27 s_bukley, p28, p29 cl, p29 tr.
Graphic elements from Shutterstock.

Artwork: Stefan Chabluk:
p7 t, p9 t, p11 b, p23 t.

Every effort has been made to clear copyright. Should there be any inadvertent omission, please apply to the publisher for rectification.

The website addresses (URLs) included in this book were valid at the time of going to press. However, it is possible that contents or addresses may have changed since the publication of this book. No responsibility for any such changes can be accepted by either the author or the Publisher.

Printed in the USA/082015/SN20150529

Library and Archives Canada Cataloguing in Publication

Mason, Paul, 1967-, author
     Your growing body and remarkable reproductive system / Paul Mason.

(Your brilliant body!)
Includes index.
Issued in print and electronic formats.
ISBN 978-0-7787-2196-3 (bound).--ISBN 978-0-7787-2210-6 (paperback).--ISBN 978-1-4271-1707-6 (pdf).--ISBN 978-1-4271-1701-4 (html)

     1. Generative organs--Juvenile literature. 2. Human growth--Juvenile literature. 3. Puberty--Juvenile literature. 4. Developmental biology--Juvenile literature. I. Title.

QM401.M37 2015   j612.6   C2015-903168-0
                                        C2015-903169-9

Library of Congress Cataloging-in-Publication Data

Mason, Paul, 1967-
 Your growing body and remarkable reproductive system / Paul Mason.
     pages cm -- (Your brilliant body!)
 Includes index.
 ISBN 978-0-7787-2196-3 (reinforced library binding : alk. paper) --
ISBN 978-0-7787-2210-6 (pbk. : alk. paper) --
ISBN 978-1-4271-1707-6 (electronic pdf : alk. paper) --
ISBN 978-1-4271-1701-4 (electronic html : alk. paper)
1. Human reproduction--Juvenile literature. I. Title.

QP251.5.M37 2016
612.6--dc23
                                        2015015361

CONTENTS

The smallest part of an organism is a cell. The cells in your body contain a structure called DNA, which you inherit from your parents.

DNA is a code that tells every cell what its job is. These are muscle cells. The DNA is contained in each cell's nucleus.

Cells join to form tissue and organs—or develop in other ways—according to DNA's instructions.

Organs work together in systems. The uterus is an organ in the female reproductive system.

A NEW HUMAN

What does your birthday mean to you? For most people, it means presents, perhaps a party, and hopefully everyone being nice to you. But have you ever really thought about what your birthday IS? It's a celebration of the exact day when you—a new human— entered the world.

The cycle of life

On the day of your birth, your journey into the world began. Human lives progress from babyhood through infanthood to childhood, then into puberty, adulthood, and, finally, old age. All living organisms— not only humans—go through this cycle of growing up and getting old before they die.

DID YOU KNOW?

Humans are mammals.

Humans belong to a group of animals called mammals. When mammals are young, they drink milk from their mothers. Other kinds of mammals include dogs, cows, sheep, monkeys, gorillas, kangaroos—and even whales and dolphins.

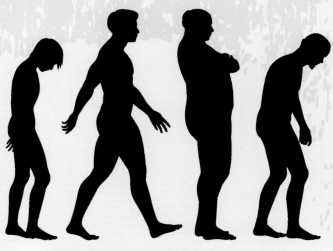

Humans are sometimes said to pass through seven stages of life: babyhood, infanthood, childhood, adolescence, adulthood, middle age, and old age.

Although a person's "birth day" is the day he or she entered the world, a human life actually starts about nine months earlier. It begins when a single cell from a man's body joins together with a single cell from a woman's. The two cells fuse into a new cell, and create something that grows and develops, until it eventually becomes a person!

Billions of birthdays

Of course, having a birthday isn't all that unusual. There are over seven billion people in the world, and every single one of us has a birthday. People die each year, but overall people are living longer. This means that the world's population is getting bigger all the time. In fact, each MINUTE it increases by 158 people.

China had the largest population in the world, at 1,355,692,576 in July 2014.

STRANGE BUT TRUE!

A baby's teeth start to form six months before it is born. Few babies are born with actual teeth, though—only about one baby in 2,000.

DON'T TRY THIS AT HOME!

Have you ever noticed that people often look like their mom or dad? The first scientist to figure out that **characteristics** are always passed on from generation to generation was Gregor Mendel. He spent years (from 1857 to 1864) growing thousands of pea plants. Mendel watched how characteristics, such as a pod's shape or color, were passed on over the years in the seeds of the plants.

It was the 1950s before scientists discovered DNA, which is what actually passes on characteristics. Without Mendel's patient pea growing, they might not have known what to look for!

WHAT MADE YOU ...YOU?

You are one crazy, mixed-up kid. Don't worry, though—it's not ONLY you. We're *all* mixed-up. This is because we are all made of a mixture of things we **inherited**, or were passed down, from our mom and dad. Our height, hair color, and other characteristics all come from our parents.

The same, but different

No one looks 100% like either of their parents. Instead, we are all a jumbled together mixture of both of our parents. The way the ingredients mix together is what makes people individuals—rather than exact copies of one another.

Siblings often look similar to each other, and similar to their parents. But siblings don't all look exactly alike. The way each sibling's characteristics combined each time their parents had a baby was a little different—so each baby looks different from the last.

STRANGE BUT TRUE!

Deoxyribonucleic acid (better known as **DNA**) is a code that determines how your body will develop. It is contained in all your body's cells, except mature red blood cells.

DNA affects your hair and eye color, which hand you write with, your height, and all the other factors that make you an individual.

Each strand of DNA is the shape of a spiraling ladder. This shape is called a double helix.

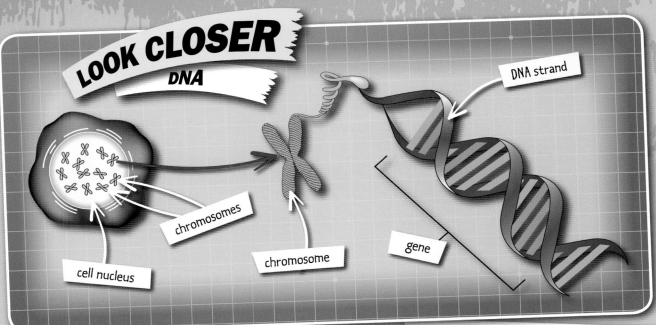

DNA strand

chromosomes

cell nucleus

chromosome

gene

Genetics

The science of how we inherit characteristics from our parents is called **genetics**. Genetic characteristics are passed on by DNA. The strands of DNA in your body's cells are like an instruction list, telling your cells how to grow and develop. Your DNA comes from both of your parents' DNA. Their instruction lists mix together, creating a completely new one just for you.

Our genes can pass on good things, such as being good at sports or having great hearing. They can also sometimes pass on bad things such as poor eyesight, or heart problems.

Anyone who has children passes on some of their characteristics through their genes. These characteristics will still be around long after the human who passed them on has died.

A forensic scientist can analyze the DNA in human hair.

DID YOU KNOW?

DNA can solve crimes.

Police forces around the world use DNA as a way of finding out who has been at the scene of a crime. DNA can be found in hair, skin, or tiny drops of blood or saliva. Just touching something may leave DNA behind!

7

THE START OF YOUR STORY

The life of every human being begins when a sperm cell from a man combines with an egg cell inside a woman. This process is known as **fertilization**. This meeting is the end of a very competitive race for the sperm cell. There isn't just one sperm trying to meet up with the egg—there are between six million and 150 million!

Expert swimmers

It's important that some sperm are expert swimmers. When the race starts, though, they have just begun to swim for the first time! Inside a man's body, sperm can't swim at all. Their swimming skills only activate as they leave.

There is only ONE winner in the sperm race. Once a single sperm has burrowed into a woman's egg, the egg's outer wall changes and no more sperm can get through.

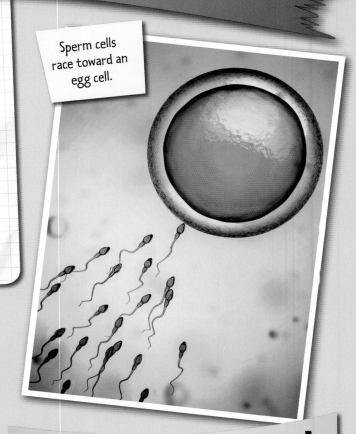

Sperm cells race toward an egg cell.

STRANGE BUT TRUE!

Before the science of fertilization was discovered in the late 1800s, some people thought that humans came preformed, contained within the tiny head of a sperm. These "spermists" claimed that women's bodies just provided a place for the sperm to grow.

A fertilized cell

Together, the sperm and egg contain all the DNA code for a new human. Scientists do not know exactly what determines which sperm gets in, but once it is inside, the egg is fertilized. The fertilized cell follows the DNA's instructions and divides. The cells divide again and again, creating a cluster of cells that roots itself in the mother's **womb**, or uterus. The cells continue to divide and change, forming an **embryo**.

STRANGE BUT TRUE!

Whether you are a boy or a girl was determined at the moment when the sperm and egg that formed you combined.

Your sex was decided by the combination of chemicals called **chromosomes** in the sperm and egg that made you. Eggs always contain the X chromosome, but sperm can have an X or Y—therefore it is sperm that determines the sex of a baby.

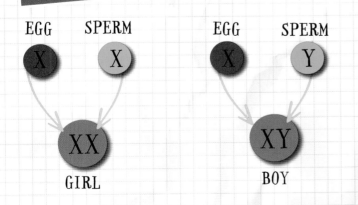

EGG	SPERM		EGG	SPERM
X	X		X	Y
XX			XY	
GIRL			BOY	

LOOK CLOSER
CELL TO EMBRYO

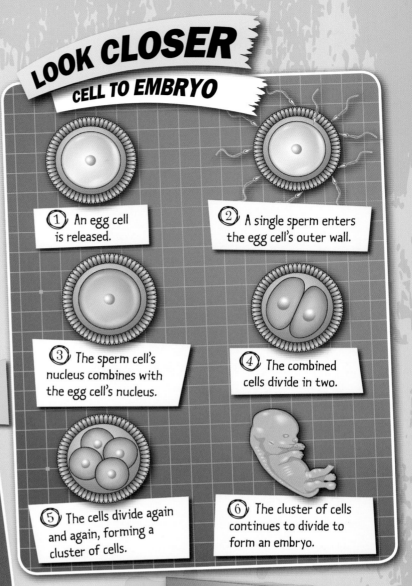

① An egg cell is released.

② A single sperm enters the egg cell's outer wall.

③ The sperm cell's nucleus combines with the egg cell's nucleus.

④ The combined cells divide in two.

⑤ The cells divide again and again, forming a cluster of cells.

⑥ The cluster of cells continues to divide to form an embryo.

DID YOU KNOW?

Not all sperm are top swimmers.

Among sperm, the best swimmers have a rounded head, a neck section behind, and a wriggly tail that they use for swimming. Sadly, studies have shown that most sperm do not achieve this high standard. Common problems include:

* a tiny head (or even two!)
* a bent neck that stops them from swimming in a straight line
* a bent, broken, or coiled tail (or even more than one), which makes swimming almost impossible.

FROM CELL TO HUMAN

Once the embryo is around eight weeks old, it becomes known as a **fetus**. Over the coming weeks and months, its limbs and organs continue to form and grow until it is ready to enter the world.

The growing fetus

The fetus grows inside a sac of **amniotic fluid**. This keeps the fetus at a comfortable temperature, and cushions it from bumps. The fetus also drinks (and then pees out) amniotic fluid. The mother's body renews the fluid about every three hours.

To grow, the fetus needs oxygen and **utrients**. It gets these from the **placenta**—a temporary organ that grows inside the mother. Nutrients and oxygen flow from the mother's blood supply to the fetus through the placenta, and along a tube called the **umbilical cord**. Waste products are also carried away through the umbilical cord. The placenta grows at the same time as the fetus. By the final weeks of pregnancy, the placenta is about one inch (2.5 cm) thick and as big as a large dinner plate.

LOOK CLOSER
A GROWING BABY

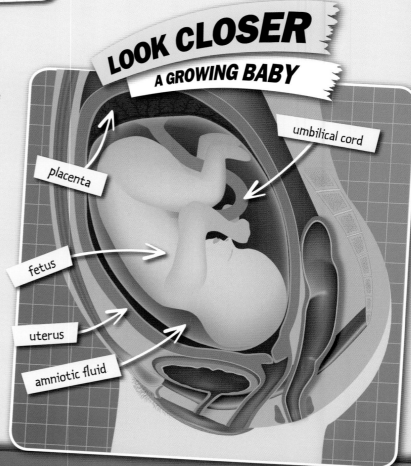

placenta

umbilical cord

fetus

uterus

amniotic fluid

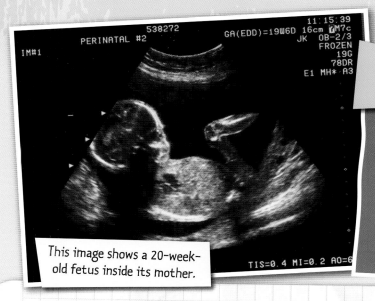
This image shows a 20-week-old fetus inside its mother.

A growing embryo or fetus changes and develops every day. Some of the key stages in the development inside the mother include:

AT FOUR WEEKS

There are just two layers of cells that have developed from the first two cells. Even so, these cells contain all the information needed to develop into a human and the amniotic sac that protects the embryo!

AT EIGHT WEEKS

At eight weeks the growing embryo becomes known as a fetus. The fetus's arms and legs grow longer and its hands and feet start to develop.

AT 12 WEEKS

At 12 weeks, the fetus's arms and legs are long and thin, and the head is about half the baby's size. The baby is around the size of a kidney bean, and has tiny webbed fingers!

AT 24 WEEKS

The fetus's lungs are developing, along with its taste buds. It is now around 10 inches (25 cm) long.

AT EIGHT MONTHS

The fetus is almost ready to be born. Even though it does not breathe on its own yet, the fetus's brain, lungs, and other organs are formed.

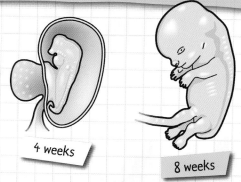
4 weeks

8 weeks

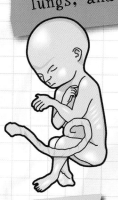
12 weeks

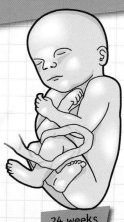
24 weeks

INTO THIS WORLD

After nine months of growing inside their mother, most babies are ready to come out into the world. In fact, babies NEED to come out. The **birth canal** to the outside world is already a tight fit. If they keep growing inside their mother for much longer, they might not fit through!

Being born

The birthing process usually takes about eight hours if it is a woman's first baby, though it can take 18 hours, or even longer! The birth of a second child often happens more quickly. There are three separate stages to giving birth:

① Contractions

First, the muscles in the mother's **abdomen** automatically start to **contract** then relax. The contractions, called **labor**, become more frequent, and more powerful. They slowly push the baby out through a tiny opening, called the **cervix**, at the bottom of the uterus. Luckily the cervix widens to help!

LOOK CLOSER

GIVING BIRTH

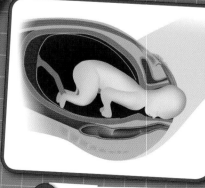

1 CONTRACTIONS

2 BIRTH

3 AFTERBIRTH

Around the world there are lots of unusual newborn baby customs.

✳ In Finland, there's been a tradition for the last 75 years of babies sleeping in cardboard boxes.

✳ Swedish babies are sometimes left outside in the cold (wrapped up and in a stroller), to help them resist illnesses later in life.

✳ In Bulgaria, some people think making a big deal about a new baby makes the Devil want to steal it. If you REALLY want to fool the Devil, you spit in the baby's eye!

② Birth

The baby squeezes down the birth canal and starts to come out head first. Its mother uses the muscles inside her body to push the baby out. Finally, it is born.

③ Afterbirth

Babies are born with their umbilical cord still connected to the placenta. Within a few minutes the cord is cut. Within an hour, the placenta also comes out of the woman's body. The birthing process is over.

STRANGE BUT TRUE!

Your **navel**, or belly button, shows where the umbilical cord connected you to your mother. People have different shaped belly buttons depending on what the cord was like, and how and where it was cut.

STRANGE BUT TRUE!

Babies have a soft gap between their skull bones to allow the skull to be **flexible** and compress in the narrow birth canal. The **protein** that stops a baby's skull from hardening until after it has been born is called "noggin"—which is also a slang word for "head."

Early birds

Babies that are born early are called **premature** babies, and may need specialist care. Most premature babies that are born a month early survive as their organs are well formed. Even babies born several months early can survive, but they may experience health problems or need special care as they grow up.

DID YOU KNOW?

Caesar gave his name to a way of being born.

Some babies cannot be born in the normal way. They may be too large to fit down the birth canal, or positioned at the wrong angle. When this happens, a small cut is made through the mother's abdomen and uterus to deliver the baby.

This is how the Roman emperor Caesar was once thought to have been born. Today, the operation is often called a cesarian or C-section birth.

TWINS: TWO TYPES

Most women give birth to a single baby. Sometimes, though, a woman gives birth to not one but TWO babies. These are called twins. If *three* babies arrive at once, they are called triplets. The record for the most babies born at once is eight—six boys and two girls. They were born in Bellflower, California, in 2009.

Are all twins the same?

No, there are two different types of twins:

✳ **Identical twins** look almost exactly alike when they are young. As they grow up, though, things like their diet and exercise affect what they look like. Even when they do exactly the same things all the time, the twins begin to look slightly different.

✳ **Fraternal twins** are born at the same time, but do not look exactly alike even when they are young.

What causes the two types of twins?

Twins develop in two different ways, which decide whether they are going to be identical or fraternal:

✳ **Identical twins** are the result of a fertilized egg (see page 9) splitting and becoming two embryos. Because they come from a single egg and sperm, the embryos have exactly the same DNA. They grow up looking confusingly alike!

Identical twins start life looking exactly alike. When they get older, it may still be hard to tell them apart.

identical twins

fraternal twins

✳ **Fraternal twins** develop when a woman's body produces two eggs at the same time. Each embryo is formed by a different egg and different sperm, so they have different DNA. They can grow up looking similar, but only as alike as brothers and sisters.

STRANGE BUT TRUE!

About a quarter of identical twins are a called "mirror-image twins." One is right-handed, the other left-handed. Their fingerprints are also mirror images of each other's.

STRANGE BUT TRUE!

A town called Cândido Godói, in Brazil, claims to be the "twins capital of the world." Between 1959 and 2008, 8% of births resulted in twins—compared to 1% in the rest of Brazil.

Cândido Godói has a rival, though. Among the Yoruba people of Nigeria, it's claimed that three of every 19 births results in twins. That means over 15% of Yoruba births produce twins.

DID YOU KNOW?

Having twins runs in the family (sometimes).

If a woman's mother or grandmother ever had fraternal twins, she is about four times as likely to have twins herself. This is because she may have inherited the possibility for her body to produce two eggs at the same time.

Having identical twins is different. It does not seem to run in families, so having identical twins is pure luck.

Fraternal twins Scarlett and Hunter Johansson

BEING A BABY

BRILLIANT BODY FACT

In Lithuania, a race is held each year to find the fastest-crawling baby!

After a baby is born, it still has a LOT of growing up to do. For example, a baby cannot see clearly right away and its brain is not fully developed. In fact, the brain—and a lot of the rest of the body—keeps on developing until the "baby" is in its 20s!

Changing babies

Lots of big changes happen during a baby's first year of life. The bones in the skull, hips, and some other parts of the body knit together. Their muscles become stronger and their control of movement becomes better. At the same time, the baby's vision and hearing improve.

New skills

As a baby's body develops, so does its brain. This means that most babies are able to learn lots of new skills during their first year:

✳ Talking

Babies start imitating noises very early in their lives. By the time they are six months old, many know basic sounds such as "ma" or "ba," but few learn the actual meaning of words before their first birthday.

✳ Moving around

Newborn babies make small, jerky movements. As their muscles develop and become stronger, their movements become more controlled. Their first lessons are to hold their heads up themselves, and to roll over. During their first year, most babies progress through sitting up to crawling around, and start to pull themselves up to standing.

STRANGE BUT TRUE!

Babies grow really quickly! In fact, it's a good thing they eventually slow down. If an average-sized baby kept on growing at the same rate it does in its first year, it would be 25 feet (7.6 m) tall and weigh nearly 308 pounds (140 kg) by the time it was 20 years old!

✳ Thinking things through

To begin with, babies don't think much about what they are doing. They cry when they are hungry or cold or need their diaper changed. As their brains develop, babies become better at working out the world around them. They start to recognize familiar voices or the sound of their own name.

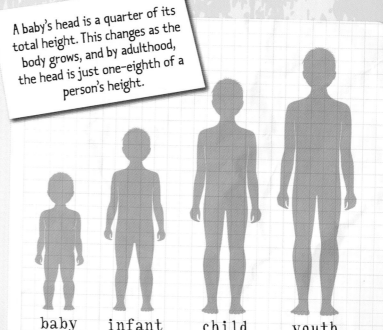

A baby's head is a quarter of its total height. This changes as the body grows, and by adulthood, the head is just one-eighth of a person's height.

baby   infant   child   youth

Babies' brains develop quickly during their first year of life.

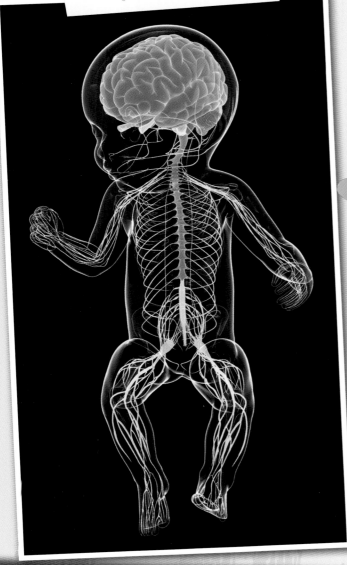

DID YOU KNOW?

Almost all babies are born with blue eyes.

Babies' eyes (like everyone's) contain a chemical that changes color when it is exposed to sunlight. If a baby has a lot of this chemical, its eyes turn brown, or even sometimes black, after it is born. If a baby has very little of the chemical, its eyes stay blue.

The exceptions to this rule are **albino** people, whose bodies do not contain the chemicals that color most people's eyes, skin, and hair.

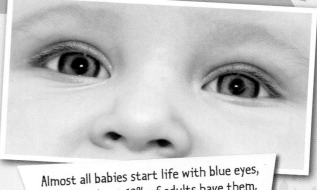

Almost all babies start life with blue eyes, but only about 10% of adults have them.

FROM TODDLING TO CHILDHOOD

When a baby learns to walk, people usually call it a "toddler." The name comes from the fact that they "toddle" at first—meaning they can't walk very well. Once a baby starts to walk, it usually gets good at it very quickly. Toddlers learn many new skills as they grow into childhood.

Talking

From baby noises, children start making sounds that can be recognized as words. Most toddlers start to learn to talk sometime between their first and second birthdays. They can join words together to say simple things like, "Carry me." After their second birthday, they start learning more words each day: about ten a day until they are six, then up to 20 a day until they have reached a point where they can communicate easily.

LOOK CLOSER
BRAIN DEVELOPMENT

The brain's structure changes as a child learns new things.

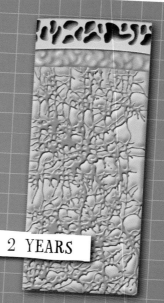

9 MONTHS

2 YEARS

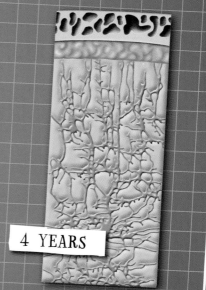

4 YEARS

Moving around

Once babies can stand up, they want to get moving. They start walking with support as they gain balance and coordination. Once they can walk, toddlers start picking things up and carrying them around—a good way to develop strength! By the time they are two, most children can run, jump, and climb. By their third birthday, few children have to think about walking or running at all—they just do it automatically.

They need a little help at first, but most babies have learned to walk by the time they are 18 months old.

Thinking things through

Sometime after their first birthday, toddlers start to work out problems. For example, they know to go to a cupboard and get a toy, even though they cannot see the toy. Their brain's ability to think things through keeps growing. By the time most children are seven, they can understand the rules of games (or bedtime, or school). By age 12, they can explain the reasons for the rules, solve problems, and are able to think about something from other people's points of view.

STRANGE BUT TRUE!

Mammals such as humans, monkeys, and gorillas need to be cared for by their parents for a long time after birth. It is years before a human baby, for example, would be able to run away from predators!

Other mammals, such as horses, cows, hippopotamuses, dolphins, and whales, are better equipped for life in the wild. They can walk or swim just hours after being born.

GROWING UP:
PUBERTY

After childhood, the next big change to a young person's growing body happens when **puberty** begins. Puberty is the physical change from childhood to adulthood. This is the time when a person becomes able to have children of his or her own.

When does puberty begin?

Puberty can start at a variety of ages. Girls often begin puberty at 11, but can be anywhere between eight to 14 years old. Boys are usually about a year behind: the average age to start is 12, but they can be anywhere between nine to 14. Puberty usually lasts for three years in girls and four years in boys, but it can vary for different people.

What happens during puberty?

When puberty arrives, chemical messengers called **hormones** start zinging around a person's body. In boys, the most important hormone is testosterone. In girls, it is estradiol.

These hormones trigger the growth of adult sex organs (see pages 22–25) and cause other changes to the body.

Changes in boys

Boys' voices change, and get deeper. They begin to grow dark body hair, particularly on their armpits and pubic area. Boys often grow rapidly taller and their muscles develop.

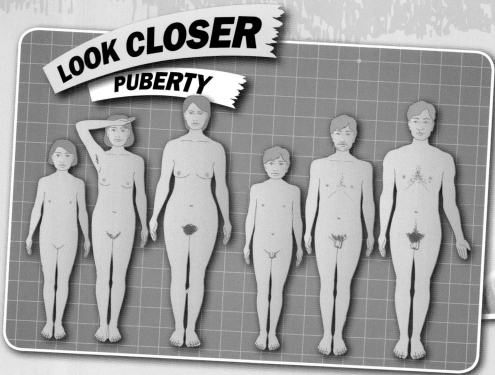

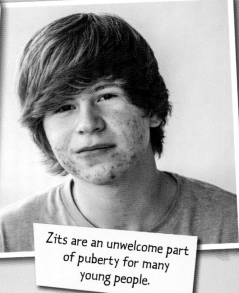

Zits are an unwelcome part of puberty for many young people.

Changes in girls

Girls' bodies start to look like an adult woman's. Their breasts form, hips widen, and their muscles develop. Their pubic hair grows, and they begin to have **periods** (see page 23 to find out more about these).

Once puberty is finished, a person's sex organs are fully developed.

Puberty problems

The changes to your body that happen during puberty can bring some problems. These include zits, which are caused by your skin releasing more oil; body odor, which happens because new sweat glands grow in your armpits, feet, and pubic area; and sudden changes of mood, caused by the hormones your body is releasing.

DON'T TRY THIS AT HOME!

The artist Leonardo da Vinci (1452–1519) was famous for his accurate drawings of human **anatomy**—particularly what people looked like on the inside. However, this wasn't the case with his drawings of women's bodies, which are said to look more like those of animals. Experts think this was because no one would let Leonardo have female bodies to **dissect**!

FEMALES AFTER PUBERTY

When a female has finished puberty, her sex organs are fully formed and her body is capable of having children. Once her ovaries begin releasing egg cells, she may become pregnant if she has sexual intercourse.

Female sex organs

A female's sex organs are made up of two key parts:

✳ **The ovaries** are two storehouses for egg cells. From each ovary, a passage called a **fallopian tube** leads to the **uterus**.

Each month a single egg is released from one of the ovaries—it is believed they alternate. Each woman is born with hundreds of thousands of egg cells. This number decreases as they get older. By the time women are old enough to have children, most have about 34,000 egg cells. Only about 400 of these will ever be released.

✳ **The uterus** is the space where a fetus grows when a female becomes pregnant. Normally the uterus is the size of an adult's fist—but it has to be able to stretch enough for a baby to fit inside. The uterus can expand to 20 times its regular size when a woman is pregnant.

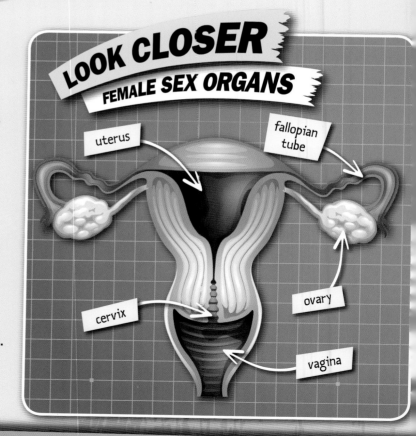

LOOK CLOSER
FEMALE SEX ORGANS

uterus

fallopian tube

cervix

ovary

vagina

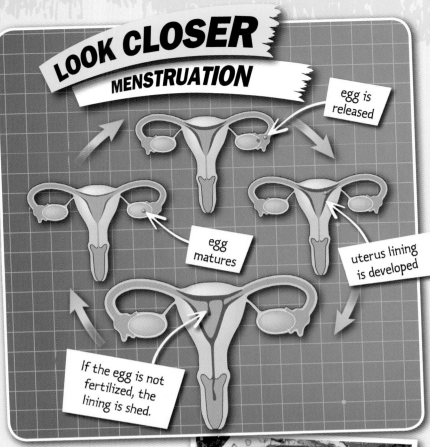

egg is released

egg matures

uterus lining is developed

If the egg is not fertilized, the lining is shed.

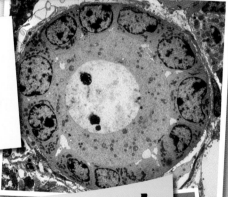

This magnified view shows a cross-section of an ovary **follicle**—the site where mature eggs are released. At the center is the nucleus of the developing egg.

STRANGE BUT TRUE!

In the past, people have come up with some odd theories about menstruating women. The ancient Roman historian Pliny the Elder claimed that a menstruating woman could stop hailstorms, lightning, and whirlwinds. He also claimed that if she walked around a field of corn, all the bugs would fall off the plants. Science today, however, has proven that there is no connection between menstruating women, the weather, or crops.

At the bottom of the uterus is the cervix, a ring of muscle. The cervix is connected to the outside world by a tube called the **vagina**. At the opening to the vagina are four folds of skin, called the **labia**.

The menstrual cycle and periods

A female can only become pregnant if an egg has been released by her ovaries. For most women, this happens roughly every 28 days. Each loop of 28 days is known as the **menstrual cycle**.

As a woman's ovary releases an egg, the lining of her uterus thickens. If she becomes pregnant, this is where the embryo will be implanted. If she does not, after a few days the thickened lining is shed. It leaves her body, along with blood and mucus, though the vagina. This is called a period.

DID YOU KNOW?

Women may have inspired the first calendars.

Many women have a menstrual cycle of 28 days. Some researchers think that this cycle may have been the basis for the first calendars developed by humans.

MALES AFTER PUBERTY

Once puberty is finished, a male's sex organs are fully developed. He is able to produce sperm, which are made and stored in the testicles. If he has sexual intercourse, his sperm can cause a women to become pregnant.

Testicles

One of the changes that happens to a male during puberty is that his testicles become able to produce sperm. The testicles are two oval organs. The average adult testicle is roughly the same size as a large walnut in its shell, though not the same shape. Usually, the right testicle is a bit bigger than the left, and the left one hangs further down.

Before birth, testicles are located inside a man's body. Following birth, they descend into a hanging skin sac called the **scrotum**. They are here because the best temperature for sperm production is 34–36°F (1–2°C) lower than human body temperature. If the testicles were inside the body, they would be too hot.

STRANGE BUT TRUE!

Most male mammals have a bone in their penises. The smallest belongs to the common shrew. Humans, apes, bulls, and horses are among the few mammals that don't have a penis bone.

a common shrew

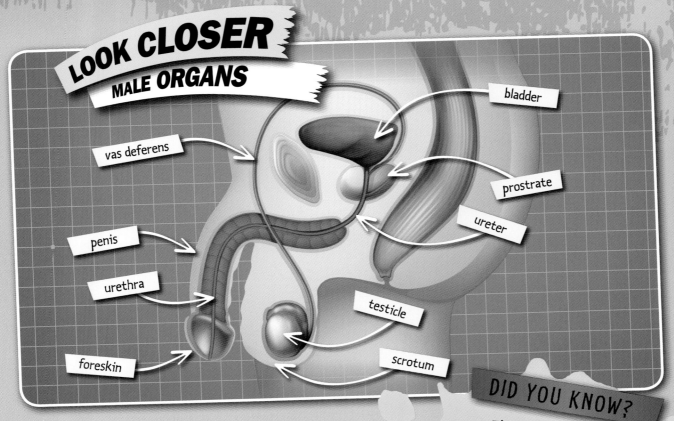

- bladder
- vas deferens
- prostrate
- ureter
- penis
- urethra
- testicle
- foreskin
- scrotum

The penis

From the testicles, a tube called the **vas deferens** loops up inside the body, then out again through the penis. The penis is used for both **urination** and reproduction. Males urinate through their penis through the **urethra**, a tube leading from the bladder to the penis.

For sexual intercourse and reproduction to happen, the penis needs to become firmer and longer. To achieve this, some of its tissue fills with blood. This is called an **erection**.

This magnified view shows a cross-section of a testicle, and the cells where sperm is produced.

DID YOU KNOW?

The average human penis is home to 42 different kinds of bacteria.

Many live under the skin that covers the tip of the penis—the **foreskin**.

Some males have the foreskin cut off, which is called **circumcision**. About 30% of the world's males are circumcised. This is usually for religious reasons, but there can be medical reasons, too.

STRANGE BUT TRUE!

Testicles have their own temperature-control system. On a hot day, the scrotum hangs down loosely. This keeps the testicles out in the air, as far away from the body's heat as possible. On a cold day, the scrotum tightens up and bring the testicles closer to the warmth of a man's body.

GETTING OLDER

Your body does not stop developing after puberty. Your bones continue to get stronger and your muscles get larger. Your vision, hearing, and **reaction times** may improve as you reach your 20s. Most people reach their "physical peak"—the time when their body is working as well as it ever will—in their 20s or early 30s.

Post-peak changes

Once peopel have reached their physical peak, they should be able to stay there for many years. This depends partly on whether they eat well and exercise enough. For example, someone who exercises regularly should be as strong at 50 as they were at 30. There are some changes, though, that happen to almost everyone.

LOOK CLOSER
BONE AND JOINT PROBLEMS

These two joint problems can affect anyone, but are most common among older people.

healthy joint

osteoarthritis joint

joint becomes less cushioned

healthy bone

osteoporosis bone

bone structure becomes weaker

Osteoarthritis causes pain in the joints.

Osteoporosis causes bones to break more easily.

* In your 30s, your hearing and eyesight usually start to weaken.

* In your 40s and 50s, your bones start to become weaker, and your heart is not able to beat as quickly. Women experience **menopause**. This is when the uterus lining stops forming and women no longer have periods. Their body stops releasing eggs, and they can no longer have children. Men's bodies become less able to produce plenty of healthy sperm.

* From their 60s onward, many people's physical and mental abilities noticeably decline. In particular, their memory gets worse, their joints become less flexible, and their heart and lungs are no longer able to work as hard.

STRANGE BUT TRUE!

Many people's mental powers decline as they get older, which makes it harder for them to learn new skills. As a result, some older people find it difficult to adapt to new technology. This cannot be said of Olive Riley from Australia, who is thought to be the world's oldest blogger—at 108 years old!

These changes do not affect everyone equally. How we age is another part of being an individual. Two things decide how your body will decline as you get older: your genes and your lifestyle. Find out more about both of these on the next page.

Tony Bennett

DID YOU KNOW?

Getting older isn't all bad!

Some people don't look forward to aging, but others have used this time for their greatest achievements.

People are capable of outstanding work as they get older. The famous philosopher Immanuel Kant wrote his greatest books between the ages of 60 and 80.

Older athletes have set some amazing records—like 73-year-old South African Otto Thaning, who swam the English Channel in 2014.

Age does not stop entertainers and musicians. In 2009, singer Tony Bennett became the oldest musician to top the Billboard chart in the United States—at 85!

STAYING FIT AND HEALTHY

If you leave a bicycle out in the rain, never put oil on its chain, and just drop it on the ground when you get off, it won't last very long. But if you look after a bike, it lasts for years. Your body is the same. If you take good care for it, it works better and lasts much longer.

Genetic influences

Your genes are the instructions that tell your body how to grow. You inherited them from your parents. A lot of what happens to your body as you get older is controlled by your genes. They influence everything, from whether a man goes bald to a person's chances of developing some diseases. At the moment, there is nothing you can do about your genes—so if your dad is bald, enjoy your hair while you have it!

Lifestyle choices

How you live your life has a BIG influence on how well your body works when you are young, and as you enter old age. If you want to live to be healthy at 100 (or more), here are three key pointers:

✳ Eat well

As your body is growing, it needs the right kinds of nutrients to become healthy and as strong as possible. Eating the right foods gives your bones, muscles, brain, and the rest of your body everything it needs to stay healthy. Avoid eating a lot of fatty or sugary foods as they can lead to serious health problems.

Vegetables and protein are an important part of a balanced diet.

☀ Do exercise

People who exercise regularly live longer than those who don't. They are also able to do more, especially as they get older. But you do not have to wait until you are older to benefit from exercise. There's lots of evidence that getting in better shape helps kids improve at school, too!

☀ Avoid things that are bad for you

Drinking alcohol, smoking cigarettes, and taking drugs have all have a bad effect on people's bodies. They affect the brain, heart, lungs, and other organs.

STRANGE BUT TRUE!

Even when he was an old man, former President Harry S. Truman was lively and full of energy. He claimed this was because every day he walked one mile (1.6 km) before breakfast.

DID YOU KNOW?

Genetic diseases may soon be curable.

Some diseases, such as breast cancer, seem to run in families. Today, scientists are researching which genes trigger these illnesses. In the future, they may be able to remove or adapt the gene to prevent some illnesses from happening.

Fauja Singh is believed to be the world's oldest marathon runner—he began running marathons in his 80s and finally put away his running shoes at the age of 101.

GROWING WORDS!

Note: Some boldfaced words are defined where they appear in the book.

abdomen The part of the body containing the digestive organs located between the bottom of the ribs to hips

albino A person or animal who does not have any coloring because they lack pigment in the body

anatomy The study of the structure and parts of the human body

birth canal The passageway between the uterus and vagina through which a baby is born

characteristics Features that help distinguish an individual

chromosome A thread-like structure, made of DNA, that is contained in the nucleus of body cells

contract To pull together

dissect To cut apart structures of an organism to investigate its anatomy

DNA The genetic code that determines how your body will develop. DNA is contained in the nucleus of body cells, and is inherited from your parents.

embryo A collection of cells that developed from a fertilized egg before the development of major organs

fertilization The moment when a female egg and a male sperm combine

flexible Able to bend easily

hormone A chemical messenger that triggers actions within the body

nutrients The substances needed by living things for nutrition, repair, and growth

premature Early

proteins Chemicals within the body, which do lots of different jobs. Among the most important jobs are triggering chemical reactions inside the body, protecting against sicknesses, carrying messages, and helping transport material around the body.

reaction time The time it takes to respond to something

sexual intercourse The act that may lead to a female becoming pregnant. During sexual intercourse, the male's penis goes into the female's vagina, then releases sperm.

urination The body's way of getting rid of some of its liquid waste products

uterus A pear-shaped female reproductive organ where a baby develops before birth, also called a womb

GROWING YOUR MIND

Would you like to grow more knowledge about your body and reproductive system? Here are some good places to find out more:

BOOKS TO READ

Hyde, Natalie. *Traits and Attributes,* Crabtree Publishing, 2009

Parker, Steve. *The Reproductive System*, Heinemann-Raintree, 2009

Prior, Jennifer. *The Human Life Cycle*, Teacher Created Materials, 2012

Rooney, Anne. *Your Physical Body: From Birth to Old Age*, Heinemann-Raintree, 2013

WEBSITES

http://kidshealth.org/kid/grow/

This website is a good place to find out about the human body. It has lots of articles on puberty and growing up.

www.amnh.org/explore/ology/genetics

The Musuem of Natural History's Gene Scene website has all sorts of information for kids on genetics including games and hands-on activities.

PLACES TO VISIT

In Boston, Massachusetts, the **Hall of Human Life** at the **Museum of Science** has over 70 interactive exhibits about how the body works. The museum is located at:

Museum of Science
1 Science Park
Boston, MA 02114
www.mos.org

The **Museum of Science and Industry** in Chicago, Illinois, features YOU! The Experience, a permanent exhibition celebrating human life. The museum is located at:

The Museum of Science and Industry
5700 S. Lake Shore Drive
Chicago, IL 60637
www.msichicago.org

In Columbus, Ohio, the **Center of Science and Industry** explores the human body in their exhibition Life: The Story of You. The museum is located at:

Center for Science and Industry
333 W. Broad Street
Columbus, OH 43215
www.cosi.org

INDEX

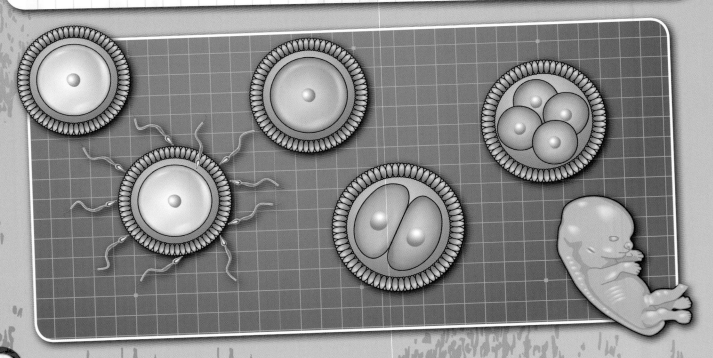